THE ADDICTION RECOVERY JOURNAL

THE
ADDICTION
RECOVERY
JOURNAL

Guided Prompts, Practices,
and Encouragement for Living with
Addiction and Preventing Relapse

NATALIE FEINBLATT, PsyD

R

ROCKRIDGE
PRESS

As of press time, the URLs in this book link or refer to existing websites on the internet. Rockridge Press is not responsible for the outdated, inaccurate, or incomplete content available on these sites.

First Rockridge Press trade paperback edition 2022

Rockridge Press and the Rockridge Press logo are trademarks or registered trademarks of Callisto Media Inc. and/or its affiliates in the United States and other countries and may not be used without written permission.

For general information on our other products and services, please contact our Customer Care Department within the United States at (866) 744-2665, or outside the United States at (510) 253-0500.

Paperback ISBN: 978-1-68539-335-9

Manufactured in the United States of America

Interior and Cover Designer: Stephanie Mautone
Art Producer: Hannah Dickerson
Editors: Andrea Leptinsky and Milena Prinzi
Production Editor: Dylan Julian
Production Manager: Riley Hoffman

Illustrations © Medialoot/Creative Market

10 9 8 7 6 5 4 3 2 1 0

This journal belongs to:

_____

CONTENTS

INTRODUCTION

The fact that you're reading these words means that you've taken a huge step forward on your journey to addiction recovery. So, congratulations! I'm Dr. Natalie Feinblatt, and as a licensed clinical psychologist and addiction treatment specialist, I know that recovering from an addiction is a daunting task. Please take a moment to acknowledge that being here is a big deal. I started working in addiction treatment early in my training. Since then, I've made it a big part of my work, due to my passion for helping those with addictions. I've worked at all levels of care, from detox on down, and with many different types of addictions. Over the years, my clients and I have used lots of books and workbooks to enrich their experience in therapy. As helpful as some books have been, I've often wished there had been accompanying guided journals to deepen the work. So, it's no surprise that I jumped at the opportunity to write this one. Although it isn't a replacement for professional help or "rehab," this journal is a wonderful way to support your recovery. In this journal, I've pulled from the many different healing modalities I've been trained in and exposed to over the years. As a result, this book is a comprehensive addiction recovery resource. No matter where you are in your recovery right now, working through whatever type of addiction, this journal will position you to better face the challenges ahead.

HOW TO USE THIS BOOK

This guided journal is divided into six sections that are each focused on key topics in addiction recovery. The various sections will help you understand your addiction, explore stress and trauma, manage difficult thoughts and feelings, build healthy relationships, navigate high-risk situations, and establish a lifestyle that will protect against relapse. Each section will contain many different prompts with space to respond in writing. You will also find plenty of exercises, practices, and affirmations throughout. Some of the material in this book may be triggering, but the journal itself is designed to help you explore those triggers and deal with them in the most healthy and effective way possible. The words "sobriety" and "substances" are sometimes used in this book, but it's designed to help with any type of addiction. You can work this journal from start to finish, or jump around to meet whatever your needs are at the time. This journal can be used alongside or after its companion piece, Althea Press's *The Addiction Recovery Workbook* by Dr. Paula Freedman, but these books are also designed to function as stand-alone titles. All that being said, there's pretty much no wrong way to use this journal. Make it your own and use it to bolster and strengthen your recovery. Whether or not you believe it right now, you deserve it.

ONE

Understanding Your Addiction and Recovery

The first part of this journal will help you focus on understanding your addiction and the beginning of your path to recovery. Think of this section like building the foundation of a house. You need a sturdy foundation to build a strong and desirable house. The prompts you'll find in this section are designed to help you stand on firm ground in your recovery from this point forward. The journal elements in this section will help you explore what addiction has looked like in your life, how your addiction developed, and why you're moving in the direction of change. You will also get clarity on what recovery looks like for you, and how you will manage it through the turbulence that is inevitable along the way. This section will assist you in getting clarity when looking back, as well as when looking ahead from here.

Addiction can have so many causes, both internal and external. A nearly infinite and highly individualized combination of life stressors and genetics can cause an addiction to develop. When you look back at the start of your issues, what internal and external factors do you think came together to cause your addiction?

_____

_____

_____

_____

_____

_____

_____

_____

_____

_____

_____

_____

_____

_____

_____

_____

_____

_____

SPECIFICS OF YOUR ADDICTION

This checklist of criteria for substance use disorder from the *DSM-5* (the primary manual used to assess and diagnose mental health disorders) will help you see exactly how addiction has been showing up and impacting your life.

Check off those items that describe your substance use or addictive behaviors over the past six months:

- ☐ You were taking more of the substance than you originally planned to take.

- ☐ You were using the substance over a longer period of time than you intended to.

- ☐ You wanted to cut down or stop but struggled to do so.

- ☐ Your use interfered with your ability to fulfill roles and responsibilities.

- ☐ You continued to use despite it causing social problems.

- ☐ You used during physically or emotionally dangerous situations.

- ☐ You developed a tolerance, needing more of the substance to get the desired effect.

- ☐ When you stopped using the substance, you developed withdrawal symptoms.

A hallmark of addiction is loss of control over behavior. No matter how hard you want to change, or how often you try, you cannot do it. Many people experience demoralization when faced with trying to make a change and not being able to. How bad did your loss of control become before you were ready to seek sobriety?

Addictions shift and change before becoming a crisis in someone's life. It helps to look at how your addiction morphed over the years, because you can gain insight into what red flags to look out for should they pop up again later. How did your addiction develop over time?

_____

_____

_____

_____

_____

_____

_____

_____

_____

_____

_____

_____

_____

_____

_____

Different cultures have a variety of ways of looking at addictions. There's a large spectrum from total denial and moral shaming at one extreme to acceptance of addiction as a disease and openness to treatment at the other. How does your culture view addiction? How has that influenced your journey thus far?

ALL ADDICTIONS ARE LIFE AND DEATH

A body scan can drive home the reality that all addictions are potentially fatal, and this can help you recognize the importance of recovery.

Starting with the bottom portion of your body and working your way up, take a moment to sit with each part of your body. Listen to what the parts have to say about your addiction. This may pop up as physical sensations, emotions, thoughts, or any combination thereof. Some things that may come up include:

☐ Has alcohol harmed your liver?

☐ What has stress done to your heart?

☐ Have drugs affected your lungs, nose, skin?

☐ What suppressed emotions have wreaked havoc in your brain?

As difficult as it may be, listen to what your body has to say about your addiction.

Denial is another key element of addictions. It keeps you in the dark about the reality of your situation and makes it hard to step into recovery. What role has denial played in your addiction story so far? How might it continue to pop up during your recovery process?

I didn't cause my addiction, I can't cure it, and I cannot control it by myself.

"It's not about what it's about" can be a helpful saying to apply to addiction. When you look closely, you realize that addictions aren't about substances or behaviors. They are about deeper underlying emotions, stressors, and coping strategies. What is your addiction about when you explore more deeply beneath the surface?

Addictions can help people relax, experience pleasure, or become numb. If these sound familiar, it's good to get specific on what using did for you. Recognition can help you find healthier coping skills to better meet your needs. How much of your addiction was driven by relaxation, pleasure, and/or numbing?

_____

_____

_____

_____

_____

_____

_____

_____

_____

_____

_____

_____

_____

_____

_____

_____

_____

Addictive behavior typically repeats the same cycle over and over. It looks like this: emotional trigger, craving, relapse, guilt, and back to emotional trigger. Can you describe how this cycle typically plays out for you? Do you have hope that this cycle can be interrupted in the future?

◢◣◢◣ DROPPING THE SHAME AND STIGMA

The shame and stigma of addiction will only hinder you. Use this meditative practice to move from their darkness into the light of recovery.

If possible, find a place outside in the sun and make yourself comfortable.

1. Use your imagination to visualize the dark energies of shame and stigma in and around you.

2. With your mind's eye, imagine that the brightness and warmth of the sun are breaking shame and stigma up and sending them down into the earth below you.

3. Take as much time as you need to see and feel shame and stigma leave you completely.

4. You can engage in this practice multiple times if necessary.

5. If weather or outdoor access is an issue, try doing this in the shower, and imagine the water washing shame and stigma down the drain.

I'm not just getting sober. I'm an active participant in my own emotional and physical recovery.

Abstinence can be achieved with substances and behaviors you can live without, but harm reduction is more appropriate for things or behaviors you cannot escape entirely. Which direction are you heading in your recovery? Why do you feel it's the best path for you at this time?

_____

_____

_____

_____

_____

_____

_____

_____

_____

_____

_____

_____

_____

_____

_____

_____

_____

"The opposite of addiction isn't sobriety. It's connection."
—JOHANN HARI

This quote highlights that addiction isn't about substances or behaviors; it's about deeper unmet needs. Whether it was connecting with others or yourself, how did your addiction rob you of true connections? How do you plan to heal those connections in sobriety?

Sobriety alone doesn't fix everything that's wrong with your life. But without the foundation it provides, you cannot begin to heal effectively in other areas. What other parts of your life are you hoping to bring healing to now that you've begun your sobriety journey?

_____

_____

_____

_____

_____

_____

_____

_____

_____

_____

_____

_____

_____

_____

While starting out on this path, I am open to taking direction and remaining teachable.

Some experience a "pink cloud" of positive feelings when recovery starts. Although it feels good at first, there is inevitably some disappointment when life stressors rear their heads again. Have you experienced a pink cloud? How has it impacted your recovery, and what was it like when it went away?

_____

_____

_____

_____

_____

_____

_____

_____

_____

_____

_____

_____

_____

_____

_____

THE WHYS AND HOWS OF YOUR RECOVERY

Let's solidify your commitment to recovery by getting concrete about why you want to recover and how you plan to go about healing.

1. Begin by listing at least three specific reasons why you have become dedicated to recovery.

   • I'm committed to my recovery because _____
   _____.

   • I'm committed to my recovery because _____
   _____.

   • I'm committed to my recovery because _____
   _____.

2. Drill down on at least three ways you are currently acting on this commitment with actual behaviors.

   • I'm acting on my commitment to recovery by _____
   _____.

   • I'm acting on my commitment to recovery by _____
   _____.

   • I'm acting on my commitment to recovery by _____
   _____.

3. If you haven't already begun to do so, it's time to turn your commitments into actions.

Recovery is not a solely intellectual pursuit, something you can think your way through without taking any notable or uncomfortable actions. Which parts of your sobriety have you thought through, and which parts have you taken action on? What future actions will you need to take to keep your recovery going?

_____

_____

_____

_____

_____

_____

_____

_____

_____

_____

_____

_____

_____

_____

Some people get tripped up on figuring out how to explain their sobriety to other people. The truth is, you don't owe anyone an explanation for your sobriety, and everyone isn't entitled to that information. How do you plan on discussing—or not discussing—the reasons for your sobriety with others?

I get to disclose my recovery to other people on my timetable, not theirs.

ADDITIONAL RECOVERY RESOURCES

It's time to think about knowing when you might need more help with your recovery journey, and what that help could look like.

1. Begin to brainstorm red flags that might pop up to indicate you need more support in your sobriety. What stumbling blocks might prove too big for you to tackle on your own?

2. Go online to research the following resources so you know what else is available should those red flags start flying. (Also consider the Resources and References sections at the back of this book on pages 161 and 162.)

   - Addiction recovery books or workbooks

   - Peer support groups for addiction recovery

   - Outpatient therapy for addiction

   - Intensive outpatient programs for addiction

   - Partial hospitalization programs for addiction

   - Residential treatment centers for addiction

   - Medical detoxification programs for addiction

3. Keep the results of your research somewhere easily accessible.

TWO

Exploring Chronic Stress, Trauma, and the Nature of Relapse

Now that you have a solid understanding of addiction and the beginnings of your recovery, it's important to explore chronic stress, trauma, and their relationship to relapse. Please know that when you are looking into these topics, you're not planning *to* relapse . . . you're planning *for* a relapse. You're making sure that you understand what factors can lead to relapse and how to head them off before they become overwhelming. Relapse doesn't have to be a part of your recovery story, and looking into the roles trauma and chronic stress may play in your life can help prevent relapse from happening. In this section, you will encounter journal elements designed to assist you in understanding how stress and trauma have influenced your addiction, and how you can manage hidden triggers with more success. These may be tough topics to dive into, but doing so will pay off down the road in your recovery.

Stress is being overwhelmed or unable to cope with mental or emotional pressure. It can come from many sources and affect individuals differently. Understanding where your stress comes from is a great place to begin in heading off relapse. What things in your life cause you the most stress?

I can handle relationship
stress without
turning back to my
addictive behaviors.

Many people with addiction are also perfectionists. Perfectionism can take the form of hyperfocus on excelling at everything, or paralyzed procrastination and a desire to be the biggest mess possible. Either route can be a significant source of stress. How does your perfectionism manifest, and how much does perfectionistic stress affect you?

Trauma is any actual, threatened, or witnessed death, injury, or sexual violence. All types of abuse—physical, sexual, verbal/emotional—are also trauma. Trauma can lead to post-traumatic stress, which is lingering emotional or physical distress caused by what happened. Was your addiction an attempt to medicate away post-traumatic stress?

_____

_____

_____

_____

_____

_____

_____

_____

_____

_____

_____

_____

_____

_____

_____

_____

Your nervous system is conditioned to respond to trauma with fight, flight, freeze, or fawn reactions. If you've experienced trauma, it's likely that you fought back, ran away, froze in place, or complied with the perpetrator of your trauma. Regardless of how you reacted at the time, can you understand and forgive yourself for how your nervous system caused you to act?

🏔 EXPLORING SAFETY

Knowing safety can be a helpful recovery tool. Use this meditation to see whether you can identify safety within yourself.

1. Find a quiet and comfortable place.

2. Take a moment to slow your breathing and relax your muscles.

3. Close your eyes, or leave them open with an unfocused gaze.

4. Look and feel inward to locate safety in your mind and/or body.

5. Take as long as needed.

6. If you can locate safety, focus on it. Where do you feel it most? What would make it easy for you to return to it in the future?

7. If you cannot locate safety, explore what *could* make you feel safe. What physical sensation or mental location might help you start building an internal sense of safety?

When you are in your "window of tolerance," you're likely able to function effectively. However, when stress throws you out of your window, it is more likely that you will become distressed, dysregulated, and agitated, or conversely become numb, detached, and dissociated. Which direction do you tend to go when stressors become overwhelming?

_____

_____

_____

_____

_____

_____

_____

_____

_____

_____

_____

_____

_____

_____

_____

_____

Exploring my past isn't about blame. It's about understanding, healing, and moving forward.

"You're only as sick as your secrets" means that the more things you keep in the dark, the worse your addiction gets. Bringing your secrets out into the light is important for addiction recovery. How have your secrets been keeping you sick? What secrets do you want to get off your chest?

_____

_____

_____

_____

_____

_____

_____

_____

_____

_____

_____

_____

_____

_____

_____

_____

🏔 ARE YOU ALSO AN ACOA?

Adult children of alcoholics (ACoAs), or of parents with any addiction, deal with unique issues that are important to understand and get support for. Even if they are in recovery now, if one or both of your parents struggled with an addiction during your childhood or teen years, it's time to try a support group meeting with others who've had the same experience. You deserve the help and healing around your specific issues that are available at these meetings.

Look into the peer support group programs listed here and consider whether you could benefit from trying out any of their meetings:

- Adult Children of Alcoholics & Dysfunctional Families support groups:
  adultchildren.org

- Al-Anon support groups:
  al-anon.org

- Nar-Anon support groups:
  nar-anon.org

- Families Anonymous support groups:
  familiesanonymous.org

I embrace both my ongoing struggles and my addiction recovery successes at the same time.

Coping skills aren't designed to make you feel better. They help you get through painful emotions in a more balanced and healthy way. It's nice if they also happen to make you feel better, but that's not their main purpose. What coping skills are currently helping you most? How have these skills changed over time?

_____

_____

_____

_____

_____

_____

_____

_____

_____

_____

_____

_____

_____

_____

_____

_____

_____

_____

Reminding yourself of insights and lessons you've learned in your life journey can be a powerful coping skill during times of emotional pain. What are some of the most important lessons and insights you've learned thus far? If you could write them for your inner child, what would they be?

_____

_____

_____

_____

_____

_____

_____

_____

_____

_____

_____

_____

_____

_____

_____

_____

_____

_____

_____

_____

_____

_____

_____

_____

_____

_____

_____

_____

_____

_____

_____

_____

_____

_____

_____

_____

_____

_____

_____

⛰ SUDS AND SURS

Use the SUDs and SURs scales at different times to rate your emotional distress and, conversely, your sense of grounded-ness. Practicing using these scales over time will increase your skill at identifying your inner states and give you insight into your emotional needs.

Circle where you are right now on the SUDs and SURs scales, and then return to them as needed in the future.

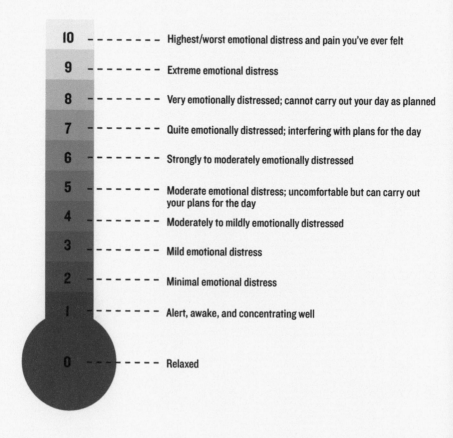

10	Highest/worst emotional distress and pain you've ever felt
9	Extreme emotional distress
8	Very emotionally distressed; cannot carry out your day as planned
7	Quite emotionally distressed; interfering with plans for the day
6	Strongly to moderately emotionally distressed
5	Moderate emotional distress; uncomfortable but can carry out your plans for the day
4	Moderately to mildly emotionally distressed
3	Mild emotional distress
2	Minimal emotional distress
1	Alert, awake, and concentrating well
0	Relaxed

SUDs stands for "Subjective Units of Distress." All hospital rooms have a "rate your physical pain" scale on the wall, and the SUDs scale is the emotional equivalent of this.

SURs stands for "Subjective Units of Resourcing." This counterpart to the SUDs scale helps you rate how emotionally healthy, grounded, balanced, and resourced you feel at any given time.

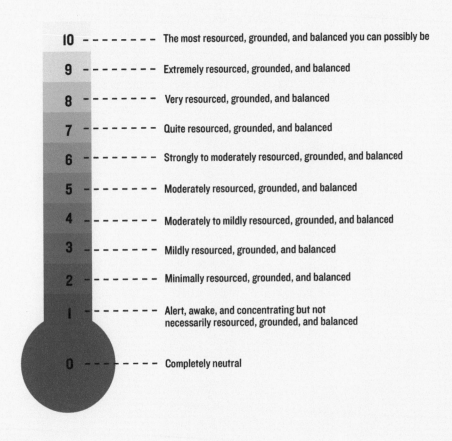

10 - - - - - - - - The most resourced, grounded, and balanced you can possibly be

9 - - - - - - - - Extremely resourced, grounded, and balanced

8 - - - - - - - - Very resourced, grounded, and balanced

7 - - - - - - - - Quite resourced, grounded, and balanced

6 - - - - - - - - Strongly to moderately resourced, grounded, and balanced

5 - - - - - - - - Moderately resourced, grounded, and balanced

4 - - - - - - - - Moderately to mildly resourced, grounded, and balanced

3 - - - - - - - - Mildly resourced, grounded, and balanced

2 - - - - - - - - Minimally resourced, grounded, and balanced

1 - - - - - - - - Alert, awake, and concentrating but not necessarily resourced, grounded, and balanced

0 - - - - - - - - Completely neutral

SCHEDULE TIME TO WORRY

Scheduling time to worry can be an effective way to reduce anxiety. It allows you to worry without it taking over your life. Trying not to worry isn't effective and only makes you worry more.

1. When you find yourself with high anxiety, say to yourself, "Not now; I'm going to worry [insert 30-minute time period]," and try to move on with your day.

2. Then, when the time comes, sit down, and let yourself worry for those 30 minutes.

3. Once the time is up, engage in an activity that's incompatible with worrying, such as singing or healthy movement to music.

4. Regularly scheduled worry time makes anxiety much more manageable.

Instead of reacting in the moment, I pause and allow myself to respond when I'm ready.

Chronic physical pain can be a unique stressor in early recovery. The substances one would turn to are no longer an option, and learning new ways to navigate the pain can be challenging. Is physical pain a part of your story? If so, how are you handling your pain alongside your newfound sobriety?

Recovery isn't linear, so it's unrealistic to expect it to continually progress upward in a straight line. It's best to expect the line to bounce everywhere, hopefully with net positive movement in the end. How nonlinear has your recovery been thus far? Are you accepting of this, or struggling with it?

_____

_____

_____

_____

_____

_____

_____

_____

_____

_____

_____

_____

_____

_____

_____

_____

_____

_____

When people relapse, they can experience the abstinence violation effect. Instead of bouncing back from a brief relapse, they figure they've already "blown it," so they might as well just keep going with the substance or behavior. How can you plan ahead to avoid the abstinence violation effect should you relapse?

_____

_____

_____

_____

_____

_____

_____

_____

_____

_____

_____

_____

_____

_____

_____

_____

_____

DEFINING RELAPSE

It's important to figure out exactly what constitutes a relapse, especially when it comes to behaviors you have to engage in regularly as a part of life.

Use the following table to help you define what a relapse would be for you. There is also space provided at the bottom for you to add and define your own challenges.

I'M IN RECOVERY FROM . . .	WHAT ABOUT . . .	MY THOUGHTS
ALCOHOL	Fermented, nonalcoholic drinks like kombucha?	
	Alcohol as an ingredient in a food recipe?	
	Nonalcoholic beer or wine?	
DRUGS	Prescriptions with addictive potential?	
	Taking more than the prescribed amount?	
	Taking someone else's prescription medication?	
GAMBLING	Spending time in a casino without gambling?	
	Making small bets with friends?	

I'M IN RECOVERY FROM . . .	WHAT ABOUT . . .	MY THOUGHTS
OVERSPENDING	Spending money on necessities? What do you consider to be necessities?	
SEX	Masturbation? Watching pornography?	
OVEREXERCISING	Taking a walk? Using a fitness tracker?	

Many triggering situations can be avoided with proactive planning—for example, choosing not to spend time with people you know will be drinking, or not watching a movie you know contains scenes of drug use, etc. What are some of your biggest triggers? How can you plan to avoid them to protect your early sobriety?

You will likely encounter triggers that couldn't have been anticipated or planned around. Life is full of surprises. You can't avoid such triggers, but you can think about how to react to them. How would you like to respond to unexpected triggers? Is there anything you can do to prepare for the unexpected?

_____

_____

_____

_____

_____

_____

_____

_____

_____

_____

_____

_____

_____

_____

_____

Cravings for substances or addictive behaviors can be surfed like waves. No wave lasts forever; they all rise, crest, and fall. Some waves are little, and some are huge, but they all end. How can you put this wave metaphor to use the next time you experience a strong craving?

THREE

Managing Difficult Thoughts and Emotions

Being able to skillfully navigate challenging feelings and thoughts is essential for success in sobriety. Given that your addiction was at least partially an emotional management tool, struggling with painful thoughts and feelings in early sobriety is inevitable. Because of this, simply trying to muscle through it won't be effective for very long. This section will present you with information and opportunities to recognize and manage your difficult thoughts and emotions in healthy ways. You can learn to do this without having to turn back to substances or addictive behaviors. The journal elements in this section are designed to help you improve your emotional intelligence through thought-provoking prompts, as well as practices and exercises focused on cognitive and emotional skill-building. The material in this section may push you outside your comfort zone—but that is where real growth happens. By the end of this section, you should feel more confident about responding to your thoughts and feelings in healthier ways.

Learning the difference between your thoughts, feelings, and behaviors is a key emotional—intelligence skill. Think of feelings as being only one or two words, whereas anything longer is a thought. And behavior is what you do. Recall a recent situation involving strong emotions and break it down into what feelings, thoughts, and behaviors were involved.

⛰ COGNITIVE DISTORTIONS

Cognitive distortions are thinking errors that cause emotional distress. When you are in emotional pain, it may be due to your thoughts being irrational, distorted, or out of line with reality.

Use the following true/false questions to determine which distortions you struggle with. Circle either "True" or "False" for each.

TRUE OR FALSE: If I relapse, my progress means nothing.

True indicates struggling with all-or-nothing thinking. Work toward seeing shades of gray instead of black or white.

TRUE OR FALSE: Mistakes at work mean I'll lose my job and become homeless.

True aligns with catastrophizing. Put effort into not blowing up small errors into disasters.

TRUE OR FALSE: Everyone is always watching to make sure I stay sober.

True indicates overgeneralizing. Eliminate "everyone," "always," and "never" from your vocabulary.

TRUE OR FALSE: My addiction is entirely my fault.

True aligns with personalizing. Put work into not blaming yourself and seeing everything as being about you.

If you have a hard time identifying your emotions, tuning into your body for somatic clues could be helpful. Tight shoulders could indicate feeling stressed, a hot back could mean anger, and a pit in your stomach might point to sadness. What physical clues can you tie to your various emotional states?

_____

_____

_____

_____

_____

_____

_____

_____

_____

_____

_____

_____

_____

_____

_____

_____

_____

It's okay to be sensitive.
Being emotional doesn't
make me "dramatic."
It makes me human.

"If it's hysterical, it's historical" means present-day big feelings that are out of proportion to the situation are often rooted in unresolved past hurts. Recognizing this and working on those old feelings leads to present-day emotional healing. Write about a recent incidence of "hysterical" feelings and their "historical" roots.

It is common to internalize adult voices you grew up around. This is beneficial when the adult voices are healthy, but it is harmful when they respond poorly to your needs. What helpful voices have you internalized? What harmful voices did you take in, and how is that affecting you today?

Did you know you can talk back to your inner critic? When it says nasty, disparaging things, you have the right to talk back respectfully ("Please don't talk to me like that") or aggressively ("Shut the f*#k up!"). Write out a dialogue between you and your inner critic.

◣◣◣ DROPPING ANCHOR

Acceptance and commitment therapy (ACT) suggests that "dropping anchor" helps you get through periods of emotional distress in a healthy and balanced way. To drop your anchor:

1. Start by acknowledging your thoughts and feelings. Notice whatever's present for you and name it: "I'm scared, overwhelmed, beating myself up, etc."

2. Get into your body. For example, do some deep breathing, stretching, healthy movement, or whatever else helps you feel your body.

3. Refocus your attention. Remind yourself of where you are and what you're doing. Name the things around you, the sounds you're hearing, or anything else about your current environment.

4. Repeat as needed.

Remember, a boat dropping anchor doesn't make the storm stop. It just helps the boat not get thrown around by the storm as much as it otherwise would have.

Sadness is a normal human emotion. Depression, however, is a debilitating mental illness that affects how you understand yourself and relate to the world around you. Write about your experiences with sadness and whether you've ever dealt with depression.

_____

_____

_____

_____

_____

_____

_____

_____

_____

_____

_____

_____

_____

_____

_____

_____

_____

Anxiety exists on a spectrum. Some anxiety is healthy and improves performance, but once it becomes excessive, anxiety negatively impacts your functioning. Where are you on the spectrum of anxiety? If you're at either end, how can you begin to move yourself toward a healthy middle ground?

I allow myself to cry
when I need to. Crying
is a coping skill.

When you're used to soothing yourself with substances or addictive behaviors, learning to self-soothe without them can be a challenge. When you are in emotional pain, how can you use your available senses to soothe yourself? What pleasurable or distracting sensory activities can you engage in?

In addition to emotional distress, it's hard to handle physical pain in early sobriety. What sorts of self-care can you use to be proactive about preventing physical pain? Once it's happened, how can you soothe yourself during physical pain so that it doesn't become a big trigger?

Anger very rarely exists on its own. Most of the time it is a response to other underlying feelings. Going deeper with your anger can help you understand yourself better and handle your anger in healthier ways. What emotions were underneath your most recent bout of anger?

I can survive feelings of grief without turning to substances or addictive behaviors.

Guilt is feeling bad because you did something wrong, whereas shame is feeling bad because you believe there is something wrong with you. Shame hinders healing from addiction. How much shame do you carry, and how does it affect your recovery?

DISTRACTION DURING EMOTIONAL DISTRESS

A dialectical behavior therapy (DBT) skill, using the acronym ACCEPTS, can help distract you from emotional pain and increase your distress tolerance.

Circle your response to each of the following questions.

1. What's a good distracting **A**ctivity?

   a. Ruminating on your upset

   b. Doing a hobby

   c. Listening to sad or angry music

2. How could you **C**ontribute to others?

   a. Do something nice for someone else

   b. Take a nap

   c. Engage in healthy movement

3. What kind of helpful **C**omparison could you make?

   a. Comparing yourself to someone you're upset with

   b. Comparing yourself to people who are "more successful" than you

   c. Comparing where you are now to where you were three months before you got sober

4. How could you distract yourself with pleasant **E**motions?

    a. Call someone to vent about your feelings

    b. Watch a funny TV show

    c. Cry for an hour

5. How could you **P**ush yourself away from your pain?

    a. Journal about it

    b. Vent to a friend

    c. Talk to a friend about their life

6. What **T**houghts could be a good distraction?

    a. Counting the colors you see around you

    b. Thinking about the current upset

    c. Thinking about a similar past upset

7. What **S**ensation could distract you right now?

    a. Going to sleep

    b. Holding an ice pack

    c. Sitting in bed staring at the wall

Answers: 1. B, 2. A, 3. C, 4. B, 5. C, 6. A, 7. B

EMOTION REGULATION WITH DBT

Practicing the DBT skill of "PLEASE MASTER" will improve your ability to regulate your emotions.

1. **Treat PhysicaL illness:** See a doctor for preventive care or to treat physical problems. Take care of your body.

2. **Balance Eating:** Honor your hunger and feel your fullness.

3. **Avoid mood-Altering substances:** In addition to staying sober, this can also include staying away from caffeine, CBD, and preworkout or herbal supplements that negatively impact your mood.

4. **Balance Sleep:** Get whatever amount of sleep you need to function well, and practice healthy sleeping habits.

5. **Get Exercise:** This can mean a formal workout program or just 20 minutes of healthy movement.

6. **Build MASTERy:** Doing something every day, big or small, that makes you feel competent can make a big difference in your mood.

Instead of fighting your emotional pain, what if you welcomed it as an ally? Your pain might have important things to tell you, or lessons to teach you, if you're willing to open up and sit with it. How might your pain be able to help you?

_____

_____

_____

_____

_____

_____

_____

_____

_____

_____

_____

_____

_____

_____

OPENING UP TO PSYCHIATRIC MEDICATION

During their recovery journey, some people realize that they need to include psychiatric medication among their coping tools.

Use the following self-inquiry process to determine whether you should investigate this avenue for yourself.

1. What thoughts and feelings come up for you at the mention of psychiatric medication?

2. Are the thoughts and feelings coming from a place of stigma, shame, or misinformation? Or are they coming from a place of balanced and honest self-assessment?

3. Notice what it feels like to take a step back and open up to the possibility that psychiatric medication could help you manage difficult thoughts and emotions.

4. Begin to consider what reg flags you would need to see in yourself for you to reevaluate your need for psychiatric medication.

Urgent feelings don't always require urgent action. Slowing myself down can be healthy.

Sometimes strong feelings can make you think you must take action, when the better path may be to wait. How can you use the following acronym to help you in these instances?

PAUSE: **P**ostpone **A**ction **U**ntil **S**erenity **E**merges

It is possible for you to carry shame that's not yours. People like your primary caregivers can project their shame onto you. You can also internalize shame and stigma from society. In addition to your own shame, who else's shame might you be carrying?

_____

_____

_____

_____

_____

_____

_____

_____

_____

_____

_____

_____

_____

_____

_____

_____

FOUR

Building Healthy Relationships

In addition to having a better relationship with yourself, addiction recovery that is successful in the long term also involves healthy relationships with other people. This section can be applied to all relationships—romantic, family, friendships, work colleagues, and with yourself. Focusing on this topic is important, because most people who struggle with addictions also have problematic relationships. They either had difficulty in this area that their addiction made worse, or their addiction negatively impacted relationships that are now in need of healing. The journal prompts in this section are designed to help you explore and improve your relationships across the board. This section includes information about communication, boundaries, assertiveness, codependency, and other topics that will help you make your relationships more balanced, peaceful, and healthy. The work you've done in previous sections has readied you to dive deeper into relationship work at this time.

Striking a balance between spending time alone and spending time with others is key. You don't want healthy alone time—solitude—to turn into unhealthy isolation. What are some of the signs that you're isolating yourself from others, and how can you go about spending more time fostering social connections?

Connection is a vital
part of my healing,
and I am worthy of
connection with others.

It's important for you to have recovery cheerleaders. These are people who both care about your well-being and make sure *you* care about your well-being. If you already know some recovery cheerleaders, write about how you can strengthen those connections. If you don't, give some thought to how you can find some.

BREATHING INTO FORGIVENESS

Using your breath to tap into your feelings about forgiveness can help you gain insight into what role forgiveness can play in improving your relationships with others and yourself.

1. Find somewhere quiet and make yourself comfortable.

2. Imagine that the word "forgiveness" is in the center of your chest.

3. Remind yourself that forgiveness doesn't mean condoning or forgetting; it just means agreeing with yourself to move forward from something that happened.

4. Begin to slowly breathe in, out, and around the word "forgiveness" in your chest.

5. Pay attention to the emotions, physical sensations, and thoughts that arise as you do this. Continue the practice for several minutes.

6. When you are done, make note of what came up for you and how it can help you decide to practice forgiveness in your relationships.

You may never get what you need from certain people. No matter how much you want it, or how much they should have it, they just don't. It's like going to the hardware store when you are looking to buy orange juice. How can you apply this concept to a relationship in your life?

Being assertive is the healthy and balanced middle between the extremes of being passive or aggressive. When you're assertive, you stand up for yourself without stomping on others. Where have you been on the passive–assertive–aggressive continuum, and how can you work to remain more in the middle?

_____

_____

_____

_____

_____

_____

_____

_____

_____

_____

_____

_____

_____

_____

Assertiveness does not involve conflict or confrontation, and I'm allowed to stand up for myself.

Since you can't control other people, boundaries aren't about telling them what to do or not do. They are about the one person you can control—yourself. What behaviors of others are you not willing to tolerate, and what are you willing to do should they cross the line with you?

_____

_____

_____

_____

_____

_____

_____

_____

_____

_____

_____

_____

_____

_____

_____

_____

You want to strike a balance between having impermeable walls and having no boundaries at all. Neither extreme is healthy, nor does it allow for functioning relationships. What is one relationship in which you can set a balanced boundary, and how can you go about doing so soon?

Although relationships with others are important, ultimately the longest and most important relationship you have is with yourself. Being able to understand, trust, and appreciate yourself and enjoy your own company is key for mental health. What is your relationship with yourself like now, and what are some ways in which it could improve?

🏔 EXPLORING CODEPENDENCY

Many people who struggle with addictions also have trouble forming and maintaining healthy relationships, or codependency. Since the overlap is high, it would be wise to determine whether this is an issue for you as well.

Use the following questions (adapted from the literature of Co-Dependents Anonymous) to see whether you struggle with forming and maintaining healthy relationships.

I see myself as completely unselfish and dedicated to the well-being of others.

1	2	3	4	5
Almost Never	Sometimes	Often	Very Often	Almost Always

I value others' approval of my thoughts, feelings, and behavior more than my own.

1	2	3	4	5
Almost Never	Sometimes	Often	Very Often	Almost Always

I am unable to identify or ask for what I need and want.

1	2	3	4	5
Almost Never	Sometimes	Often	Very Often	Almost Always

I have trouble setting healthy priorities and boundaries.

1	2	3	4	5
Almost Never	Sometimes	Often	Very Often	Almost Always

I'm extremely loyal, remaining in harmful situations for too long.

1	2	3	4	5
Almost Never	Sometimes	Often	Very Often	Almost Always

I freely offer advice and direction without being asked.

1	2	3	4	5
Almost Never	Sometimes	Often	Very Often	Almost Always

I allow addictions to people, places, and things to distract me from achieving intimacy in relationships.

1	2	3	4	5
Almost Never	Sometimes	Often	Very Often	Almost Always

If you scored 20 or higher, you likely struggle with codependency. Please check the Resources section in the back of this book (page 161) for materials that can assist you.

INTERPERSONAL EFFECTIVENESS WITH "DEAR MAN"

The next time you need to have a difficult conversation with someone, try to employ the DBT skill of DEAR MAN. You can even try writing things out with this format and practicing ahead of time.

Describe the situation and stick to just the facts

Express your feelings and opinions

Assert yourself by asking for what you want, or by saying a clear "no"

Reinforce the other person ahead of time by explaining the consequences of the situation

Mindfulness of your objectives is key; maintain your position and don't get distracted

Appear confident and competent

Negotiate by being willing to give and to get

You can also turn the issue over to the other person and ask for alternative solutions.

Instead of just saying "sorry" and moving on when you've done something hurtful, focus on making sincere amends that can repair the relationship. Admit wrongdoing without excuses, fix the situation, and show how you will change your behavior moving forward. What's an amends you need to make, and how can you do so?

When you're single, you grow in ways you can't when you're in a relationship, and when you're in a relationship, you grow in ways you can't when you're single. What's the longest time you've ever been single? What might this information show you about yourself and your relationship patterns?

When other people's drama jeopardizes my recovery, I remind myself, "Not my circus, not my monkeys."

Some people cannot be trusted to respond to your life in helpful or healthy ways. You can put these people on a "need to know" basis in your life to spare yourself emotional distress. Who might you need to shift to a "need to know" basis in your life, and why?

Life coach Cheryl Richardson said, "If you avoid conflict to keep the peace, you start a war inside yourself." Avoiding conflicts doesn't accomplish anything; it just creates more unhappiness and discord within yourself. Either way, something's got to give. What conflicts are you avoiding, and how is that impacting your mental health?

Regardless of whether other people can meet them or not, you are allowed to have needs. Having needs doesn't make you "needy." It makes you human. What are some of your emotional needs right now, and who can you connect with to try to get them met?

FAIR FIGHTING TECHNIQUES

Most of your relationships can be improved by learning and practicing some "fair fighting" techniques designed to make conflicts healthier and more productive.

Over the next two weeks, use these fair fighting techniques in daily communication to practice incorporating them into your healthy relationship skill set.

MON	TUES	WED	THUR	FRI	SAT	SUN
Stick to one topic at a time	No degrading language	Use "I" statements instead of "you" statements	Take turns speaking	No yelling	Take a time-out if things are getting heated	Don't attack areas of personal sensitivity

MON	TUES	WED	THUR	FRI	SAT	SUN
Avoid words like "always" and "never"	Don't stonewall or give the silent treatment	Only set boundaries you are willing to enforce	No use of force or physical acting out	Seek to understand the other person instead of defending yourself	Wait until you're well fed and well rested to have the conversation	Propose solutions to the problem

Reparenting your inner child is a way to improve your relationship with yourself. Give your inner child the kindness, love, and attention you didn't get growing up. Ask your inner child what they need, and write their answers in the space provided. How can you begin to reparent them using this information?

I continue to take actions that will help earn back the trust of my loved ones.

Truly listening to others isn't a passive activity. It is an active skill set. Being a good listener involves paying attention, withholding judgment, reflecting, clarifying, and summarizing. How do you typically listen to others, and how can you start to incorporate these active—listening skills into your daily interactions?

BORING AND FANCY SELF-CARE

Another way to improve your relationship with yourself is to make sure you're practicing self-care, both the "boring" and "fancy" kinds.

Over the next few days, make sure to engage in both types, either activities you think of yourself or ones listed here:

BORING SELF-CARE	FANCY SELF-CARE
Do laundry	Get a massage
Take a shower	Buy yourself something nice
Clean your living space	Go out to eat
Eat when hungry	Buy yourself flowers
Take your medication(s)	Go to a concert
Get groceries	Spend time at the beach
Make a doctor's appointment	Go for a hike
Respond to emails and texts	Go to the movies
Feed your pets	Make a vision board
Take a nap	Say affirmations

FIVE

Navigating High-Risk Situations and Environments

Moving forward as a sober person means that you will constantly be encountering situations and environments that exist on a continuum from low to high risk for relapse. When it comes to higher risk, just crossing your fingers and hoping for the best is not sufficient for protecting your recovery. You need to be proactive to navigate these things in ways that safeguard your well-being, and this section is designed to help you do just that. In this section, you will find prompts, practices, and exercises to help you plan for how to handle people, places, and things that will trigger you. An exploration of topics like your relapse prevention plan, self-sabotage, red flags, assertiveness, and coping skills will assist you in continuing your recovery in a protected way. You cannot eliminate the risk for relapse, but you absolutely have the power to reduce it.

Your relapse prevention plan is not static or set in stone. It is a living document that can (and should!) be continually edited and updated to keep up with the ever-changing nature of your recovery. There's no time like the present. Take a moment to develop a prevention plan. Update and edit your plan as needed.

_____

_____

_____

_____

_____

_____

_____

_____

_____

_____

_____

_____

_____

_____

_____

_____

🏔 CLEANING UP

One thing you can usually control is your living environment, so take some time to clear out anything that could trigger you. Have a supportive friend present with you for added protection.

1. Are there any leftover substances or paraphernalia that are still in your living space? If so, it's time to remove them entirely by whatever means necessary. Remember, sometimes people in active addiction hide things, so make sure to search thoroughly for anything that might be stashed away.

2. Are there any especially triggering things or places in your living space? If this is the case, it could be the time to do a little redecorating.

3. What about smells? Open windows and break out some air freshener or scented candles if need be.

Go through the contacts in your phone and the social media accounts you follow. Delete, unfollow, and block any people or accounts that endanger your recovery. Again, it can help to have a supportive friend assist you. Once you're done, write about the thoughts and feelings that came up during and after this process.

Almost any relapse prevention coping skill that is healthy in moderation can become unhealthy when used to an extreme. It's good to have a wide variety of tools in your tool kit. What coping skills do you use, and which ones should you watch out for in terms of using them to an extreme?

_____

_____

_____

_____

_____

_____

_____

_____

_____

_____

_____

_____

_____

_____

_____

_____

_____

Relapse dreams are normal in early recovery, and I don't let them throw me off course.

TASKS TO REDUCE THE RISK OF RELAPSE

If you haven't already, now is a great time to engage in tasks that will help reduce your risk of relapse.

1. Create or strengthen a support network, which can include your therapist, sponsor, partner, family, friends, and anyone else you'd consider part of your treatment team.

2. Recognize people, places, and things that trigger you to engage in addictive behaviors.

3. As much as is in your control, avoid situations involving drugs, alcohol, or your addictive behaviors. When these situations cannot be avoided, plan for ways to be supported and stay safe.

4. Make sure helpful resources are on hand all the time.

5. Create a daily routine focused on recovery that can consist of meditation, therapy, peer support group meetings, and/or movement.

When you find yourself in a triggering situation, remember that leaving is a coping skill. No matter what others may think or say, you are allowed to leave anything at any time for any reason without having to justify your decision. Imagine leaving a risky situation, and explore the thoughts and feelings that may come up.

UNREALISTIC BELIEFS ABOUT URGES

Recovery can be tough if you hold any beliefs about your urges that are unrealistic or inaccurate. Spotting and correcting these thoughts can benefit your sobriety.

Borrowing from the wisdom of SMART Recovery, use the following checklist to see whether beliefs about urges are endangering your recovery.

YES	NO	BELIEFS
		MY URGES ARE INTOLERABLE. Checked "Yes"? Urges make you (very!) uncomfortable, but you can tolerate them without losing your mind or dying.
		I CAN ONLY STOP MY URGES BY GIVING IN TO THEM. Checked "Yes"? Urges will always go away in time. Some are quick, some long, but they will always end on their own.
		IT'S NOT TOO BAD TO GIVE IN TO AN URGE. Checked "Yes"? Giving in to urges reinforces them and makes them stronger and harder to resist over time.
		I HAVE TO ELIMINATE MY URGES. Checked "Yes"? Urges are normal, and trying to get rid of them entirely is unrealistic.

I am willing to step outside my comfort zone to protect my recovery and prevent relapse.

Expectations are resentments waiting to happen, and resentments often lead to cravings and/or relapse. Replacing expectations with acceptance can help avoid this dangerous situation. What are some areas of your recovery in which you can move from expectation to acceptance? And what resentments are currently putting your recovery at risk?

_____

_____

_____

_____

_____

_____

_____

_____

_____

_____

_____

_____

_____

_____

_____

_____

_____

The last thing you want to do when trying to navigate high-risk situations and environments is self-sabotage. It can be hard to catch, but learning to spot when you're self-sabotaging can be key to protecting your recovery. Have you been self-sabotaging, and how can you catch and redirect yourself when you do?

The acronym WAIT (**W**hy **A**m **I** **T**alking?) can be useful in many situations, especially when you find yourself overexplaining and justifying your recovery in situations where people aren't open to listening. How can you use WAIT the next time you're in a situation that puts your sobriety at risk?

⛰ RELAPSE RED FLAGS

You must be very familiar with relapse red flags to spot and avoid or work around them.

Use this fill-in-the-blanks exercise to sharpen your ability to spot them.

1. Constantly participating in a _____ addiction such as shopping, gambling, exercising, or video games.

2. Spending time in places where you used to _____ .

3. Keeping _____ in your living space.

4. Hanging out with people who are _____ often.

5. _____ yourself from your support network and other people.

6. Starting to _____ support group meetings or therapy appointments.

7. Thinking that you _____ than the people who are trying to help you.

Answers: 1. Replacement; 2. Use substances or engage in addictive behaviors; 3. Substances or paraphernalia; 4. Drinking, using, or engaging in addictive behaviors; 5. Isolating; 6. Miss; 7. Know better

As my coping skills
increase and strengthen,
I no longer need
to self-medicate
with substances or
addictive behaviors.

INTERNAL FAMILY SYSTEMS

Developed by Richard C. Schwartz, Internal Family Systems (IFS) is a way of working with the mind that can come in handy when navigating situations that put your recovery at risk.

1. Find a quiet place to get settled and still.

2. Slow your breathing and relax your muscles.

3. Recall a situation that puts your recovery at risk.

4. Look inside for an "Exile," a part of yourself that holds painful emotions. Ask your Exile how it wants to respond to this situation.

5. Next, look inside for a "Firefighter," a part that soothes and distracts. Ask your Firefighter how it wants to respond.

6. Then look for a "Manager," a part that protects you and controls the situation. Ask your Manager how it wants to respond.

7. Finally, look for your "Self" at your core or center. Your Self is clear, compassionate, courageous, and connected. Ask your Self how it wants to respond.

Creative pursuits are great coping skills, as they are both distracting and fulfilling. You don't even have to be particularly creative or good at them to derive a benefit! What comes up for you when you consider being creative to cope with urges and triggering situations?

If you find yourself holding on to things that put your recovery at risk, remind yourself of the saying "Let go or be dragged." If you don't let go, you and your sobriety are going to get dragged . . . and may not survive. Describe applying this maxim to something that's currently putting you at risk.

_____

_____

_____

_____

_____

_____

_____

_____

_____

_____

_____

_____

_____

_____

_____

_____

If you're in recovery for multiple addictions, keep in mind that sometimes the credits don't transfer. Just because you've done work on one issue doesn't necessarily mean the healing will apply to the other(s). Write about which parts of your recovery can apply to others, and which parts might need individual attention.

If someone has a problem with my problem with my sobriety, that is their problem entirely . . . not mine!

When it comes to coping with a relapse, it's important to remember that falling down isn't the problem—staying down is. Responding to relapse with resilience is the key to keeping your recovery on track. How can you begin to plan to get back up should a relapse knock you down?

_____

_____

_____

_____

_____

_____

_____

_____

_____

_____

_____

_____

_____

_____

_____

_____

Relapses should be treated as learning opportunities, as they provide insight on how to strengthen and protect your recovery. If you've relapsed, what have you learned from that experience? If you haven't relapsed, how can you plan ahead to learn as much as possible from any future relapse?

_____

_____

_____

_____

_____

_____

_____

_____

_____

_____

_____

_____

_____

_____

_____

_____

Acknowledging your recovery accomplishments is important for keeping momentum going in the healing process. You're allowed to congratulate yourself, even if your recovery hasn't gone "perfectly." Write some positive messages to yourself about how you have handled your recovery thus far, and don't be afraid to validate your accomplishments.

Your addictive habits are well-worn trails in your brain. Recovery is creating trails where none currently exist, a process that requires patience and persistence. How have you been working to create these new neural pathways, and how can you continue to make new trails while letting the old ones grow over?

SIX

Establishing a Lifestyle to Help Prevent Relapse

It's time to incorporate what you've learned in this book into a lifestyle that will protect against relapse. No matter how much sober time you have, relapse is always a risk, which is why it is so important to create a life that supports your recovery. This section will cover topics ranging from the importance of sleep, movement, and nutrition all the way to how to incorporate mindfulness, gratitude, and hobbies into your life. Establishing healthy routines and rituals will help you stay sober by connecting you to the values that create a meaningful life. While working on this section, as well as from this point forward, remind yourself that recovery is not linear. You will continue to experience ups and downs on your path to recovery, and this section is here to help you be vigilant and flexible when faced with these expected and normal challenges.

Write about who you used to be, both the parts you want to grow past and the things you want to hang on to. Then write about who you aspire to be day-to-day and in the future. Finally, write about how you can start to bridge the gap between these two people.

ENVISIONING YOUR FUTURE

Having a firm grasp on the future you want to create helps you bring that dream into reality.

Answer the following questions to help yourself create a full and detailed vision of your future:

1. How do you want your daily life to look in the future? What is your ideal day-to-day routine?

_____

_____

_____

2. What role do career, family, and social life play in this future?

_____

_____

_____

3. How do you want to feel emotionally in this future?

_____

_____

_____

continued >

4. What sorts of thoughts do you want to be thinking in this future?

_____

_____

_____

5. How do you want to experience your body in this future?

_____

_____

_____

6. What does this future look like? What are the people, places, things, colors, and textures around you?

_____

_____

_____

7. What does this future sound and smell like?

_____

_____

_____

The plan for your recovery isn't to achieve your future goals without facing any challenges. It's how to reach those goals despite all the challenges that will inevitably present themselves. How can you create the flexibility, resilience, motivation, and acceptance you'll need to create your future despite challenges?

_____

_____

_____

_____

_____

_____

_____

_____

_____

_____

_____

_____

_____

_____

I believe in my ability to create a healthy lifestyle that protects my recovery.

SLEEP HYGIENE

Sleep can suffer during early sobriety for a variety of reasons. Incorporating good sleep hygiene behaviors will likely improve your quality and quantity of sleep.

Give these behaviors a try to see whether they improve your physical and mental health.

1. Reduce your caffeine intake and don't ingest caffeine for several hours before bedtime.

2. Take time in the evening to journal about thoughts that may keep you awake at night.

3. Stop looking at screens 30 minutes before bedtime, and keep electronic devices away from your sleeping area.

4. Make your sleeping environment cool, dark, and comfortable.

5. If you don't fall asleep right away, or if you wake up in the middle of the night, don't toss and turn in bed for more than 20 minutes. Get up and engage in a restful activity elsewhere until you feel tired enough to try sleeping again.

On average, you should drink about three liters of water daily to maintain optimal physical and mental health. How has your addiction impacted your ability to stay hydrated? What can you do to make sure that you are practicing self-care around drinking enough water daily?

_____

_____

_____

_____

_____

_____

_____

_____

_____

_____

_____

_____

_____

_____

_____

_____

Having a healthy relationship with food involves honoring hunger, feeling fullness, rejecting the diet mentality, and practicing gentle nutrition. What was your relationship with food like during your addiction? How is it different in sobriety? How can you begin to apply these tenets to your relationship with food?

_____

_____

_____

_____

_____

_____

_____

_____

_____

_____

_____

_____

_____

_____

_____

_____

Instead of forcing yourself to exercise to lose or maintain weight, it's healthier to engage in movement you enjoy to improve your mental health and physical fitness. What has your relationship to exercise looked like previously, and how can you begin to shift the focus from your weight to your overall mental and physical health?

I show my body love through movement, rest, honoring hunger and fullness, and accepting my sizes and shapes.

Sometimes people avoid peer support groups because they have misconceptions about how they work. What thoughts may be keeping you from trying a peer support group? What kind of research can you do to see whether these ideas are accurate?

DAILY GRATITUDE PRACTICE

There are copious amounts of research on how a gratitude practice can improve and maintain mental health. Try this practice daily for the next five days and see what it does for you.

1. Take three slow, deep breaths.

2. Focus on the thing you are most grateful for in this moment. Try to hold your focus here for at least 30 seconds.

3. In 30-second intervals, allow this feeling of gratitude to broaden to include:

   a) Everyone and everything in your life

   b) Your city

   c) Your state

   d) Your country

   e) The entire world

4. Write down five things you are grateful for today. Do not copy any items from the previous day's list.

5. Tell one person that you are grateful for them and why.

Many people with addictions know others with the same struggle. It can be difficult to not enable someone by protecting them from the consequences of their choices. This behavior harms, stresses, and endangers both parties. How do you know when you're enabling someone, and how can you take a step back to protect yourself and them?

Mindfulness is moment-by-moment gentle awareness of your thoughts, feelings, behaviors, and physical sensations that can be strengthened by meditations, breathing exercises, or other activities. Since mindfulness is a valuable skill for those in early recovery, how can you begin to work the muscle of your mindfulness?

_____

_____

_____

_____

_____

_____

_____

_____

_____

_____

_____

_____

_____

_____

_____

_____

Many people try one type of meditation and decide it's not for them without realizing that there are many different types of meditation. How can you gather information on what types of meditation exist? Once you have this information, how can you decide which type(s) you will try?

Therapy with an addiction specialist can be an integral part of recovery. If therapy has been a part of your journey, write about what you have gained from this type of help. If you haven't tried therapy yet, explore the reasons why and brainstorm around any financial limitations and/or misconceptions that may be getting in the way.

Different types of professional help can be useful additions to your recovery journey, either in place of or in addition to talk therapy. These can include (but are not limited to) art therapy, psychodrama, animal-assisted therapy, biofeedback, group therapy, and life coaching. Which have you tried? How were they helpful? What other types of help are you willing to explore?

◢◣◢ PROGRESSIVE MUSCLE RELAXATION

Follow this sequence of muscle tensing and releasing when-
ever you need help reducing tension in your body, coming
back to the present moment, or falling asleep.

Tense your muscles as hard as you can, hold the tension for
three seconds, and release the muscles in this order:

1. Curl your toes under your feet.

2. Point your toes and feet up toward your knees.

3. Press your thighs into the chair you're sitting in.

4. Pull your belly button back toward your spine.

5. Bring your arms up into bicep curls.

6. Make fists with your hands.

7. Press your shoulder blades back and together.

8. Bring your shoulders up to your ears.

9. Bring your chin down into your neck/chest area.

10. Squeeze your face like you're eating a lemon.

I'm allowed to be proud of my progress without having to compare myself to anyone else.

STAY BUSY WITH HOBBIES

Finding hobbies you enjoy and are passionate about can make a huge difference in the quality of your recovery journey, both present and future.

Use the following table to circle hobbies you would be interested in trying soon.

Cooking	Dance	Painting	Sports	Gardening
Video games	Geocaching	Ceramics	Drawing	Hiking
Photography	Genealogy	Interior design	Acting	Role-playing games
Creative writing	Camping	Archery	Fishing	Martial arts
3-D printing	Reading	Karaoke	Fill in your own:	Fill in your own:

When you're trying to establish a lifestyle to help prevent relapse, you don't have to do it perfectly or without breaks. Resting doesn't make you "lazy." How are you doing with giving yourself the grace to make mistakes and allowing yourself time to rest and relax during this process?

It is okay for me to feel "recovery fatigue," because I'm doing a lot of emotional heavy lifting.

When you find yourself carrying resentment around, try to "drop the rock." Resentments only weigh you down and make everything harder for *you*, not for whomever you're resentful at. It's hard to lead a healthy lifestyle while holding on to resentments. What rocks can you begin to drop today?

Substances and addictive behaviors separate you from your intuition, and your recovery journey helps you reconnect to it. When you really try to listen to your gut (and it's okay if that is still just a tiny voice that's finding its footing), what does it say about where you need to go from here?

_____

_____

_____

_____

_____

_____

_____

_____

_____

_____

_____

_____

_____

_____

_____

RESOURCES

12-STEP PROGRAMS
en.wikipedia.org/wiki/List_of_twelve-step_groups

List of over 30 different 12-step-based peer support programs that are spiritual but nondenominational.

OPEN PATH PSYCHOTHERAPY COLLECTIVE
openpathcollective.org

Nationwide directory of therapists who offer low-cost services, from $30 to $60 per session.

PSYCHOLOGY TODAY THERAPIST FINDER
psychologytoday.com/us/therapists

Search for a therapist by location (for either in-person or tele-health sessions), areas of expertise, insurance taken, and many other factors.

RECOVERY DHARMA
recoverydharma.online

A Buddhism-based peer support group for addiction recovery.

SMART RECOVERY
smartrecovery.org

Group addiction recovery support that is secular and science-based, using cognitive behavioral therapy and nonconfronta-tional motivational methods.

REFERENCES

American Psychiatric Association. *Diagnostic and Statistical Manual of Mental Disorders, Fifth Edition*. Washington, DC: American Psychiatric Association, 2013.

Co-Dependents Anonymous. "Patterns and Characteristics of Codependence." coda.org/meeting-materials/patterns-and-characteristics-2011. Accessed March 31, 2022.

Freedman, Paula A. *The Addiction Recovery Workbook: Powerful Skills for Preventing Relapse Every Day*. Emeryville, CA: Althea Press, 2018.

Hardin, Rosemary. *SMART Recovery Handbook*. 3rd ed. Mentor, OH: SMART Recovery, 2013.

Hari, Johann. "Everything You Think You Know about Addiction Is Wrong." TED Talk, 2015. youtube.com/watch?v=PY9DcIMGxMs.

Hayes, Steven C., and Kirk D. Strosahl, eds. *A Practical Guide to Acceptance and Commitment Therapy*. New York: Springer Science + Business Media, 2004.

Jacobson, Edmund. *Progressive Relaxation: A Physiological and Clinical Investigation of Muscular States and Their Significance in Psychology and Medical Practice*. 2nd ed. Chicago: University of Chicago Press, 1938.

Lindberg, Eric. "Practicing Gratitude Can Have Profound Health Benefits, USC Experts Say." November 25, 2019. news.usc.edu/163123/gratitude-health-research-thanksgiving-usc-experts.

Linehan, Marsha M. *DBT® Skills Training Manual*. 2nd ed. New York: Guilford Press, 2015.

P., Bill, Todd W., and Sara S. *Drop the Rock: Removing Character Defects, Steps 6 and 7.* 2nd ed. Center City, MN: Hazelden Publishing, 2005.

Richardson, Cheryl. *Stand Up for Your Life: A Practical Step-by-Step Plan to Build Inner Confidence and Personal Power.* New York: Free Press, 2002.

Schwartz, Richard C. *Internal Family Systems Therapy.* New York: Guilford Press, 1995.

Siegel, Daniel J., *The Developing Mind: Toward a Neurobiology of Interpersonal Experience.* New York: Guilford Press, 1999.

Substance Abuse and Mental Health Services Administration (SAMHSA). "Contact Us." samhsa.gov/about-us/contact-us. Accessed March 31, 2022.

Tribole, Evelyn, and Elyse Resch. *Intuitive Eating: A Revolutionary Anti-Diet Approach.* 4th ed. New York: St. Martin's Essentials, 2020.

Yerkes, Robert M., and John D. Dodson. "The Relation of Strength of Stimulus to Rapidity of Habit-Formation." *Journal of Comparative Neurology and Psychology* 18, no. 5 (1908): 459–82. doi.org/10.1002/cne.920180503.

ACKNOWLEDGMENTS

A big thank-you to Callisto Media and everyone there who assisted with the creation of this book.

Much love and gratitude to my husband and friends for their support while working on this project.

And thanks to everyone who helped me gather the wisdom I put into this book.

ABOUT THE AUTHOR

DR. NATALIE FEINBLATT, PsyD, is a licensed clinical psychologist in Los Angeles, California, who has worked in mental health for twenty years. She practices from a Health at Every Size and fat acceptance perspective, is LGBTQIA+ affirmative, and does not pathologize sex work, kinks, or ethical nonmonogamy. Learn more and contact Dr. Feinblatt at DrNatalieFeinblatt.com.